I Bet It Fits!

By Cameron Macintosh

I can see a hat!

I bet it fits me!

Fit, fit, fit!

It has a rip in it.

I can see ten caps.

The ten caps tip!

Tip, tip, tip!

A cat hat!

I bet it fits Sam!

Fit, fit, fit!

I can see a bat cap!

I bet it fits!

Fit, fit, fit!

CHECKING FOR MEANING

1. How many caps can the reader see? *(Literal)*

2. Who does the cat hat fit? *(Literal)*

3. Why do you think the speaker bets the hat will fit before trying it on? *(Inferential)*

EXTENDING VOCABULARY

hat	Look at the word *hat*. Can you create a new sentence using the word *hat* and a word that rhymes with it?
bet	Look at the word *bet*. What sound does it start with? What other words can you think of that start with this sound?
fits	Look at the word *fits*. What is the base of this word? What has been added to the base?

MOVING BEYOND THE TEXT

1. Why do you think the caps are tipping in the story?

2. How do you think Sam feels when the cat hat fits her?

3. How might the story change if the bat cap didn't fit the boy?

4. If you were the main character, what other type of hat would you want to try on? Why?

SPEED SOUNDS

Cc	Bb	Rr	Ee	Ff	Hh	Nn

Mm	Ss	Aa	Pp	Ii	Tt

PRACTICE WORDS

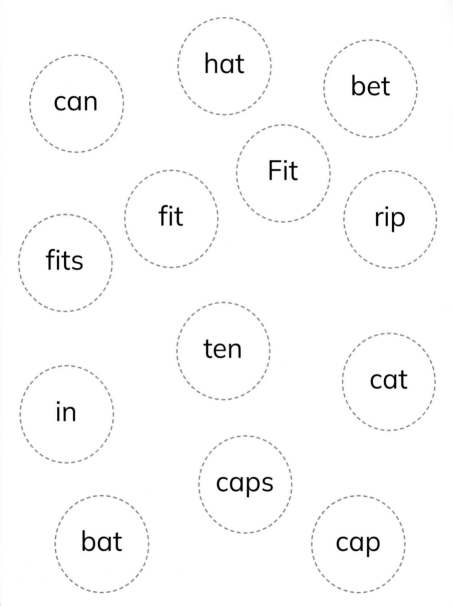

can

hat

bet

Fit

fit

rip

fits

ten

cat

in

caps

bat

cap